PERSONAL PRAYERS FOR CHILDREN

Brief simple prayers to encourage
children to talk naturally
to God every day

WIN MORGAN

DIMENSIONS
FOR LIVING
NASHVILLE

PERSONAL PRAYERS FOR CHILDREN

Library of Congress Cataloging-in-Publication Data

Morgan, Win.
   Personal prayers for children : a personal prayer book : brief, simple prayers to encourage children to talk naturally to God every day / Win Morgan.
     p. cm.
   Summary: Presents Bible verses and simple prayers arranged alphabetically by topics such as angels, country, youth, and wisdom.
    ISBN 0-687-09916-1 (alk. paper)
    1. Children—Prayer-books and devotions—English. [1. Prayers. 2. Christian life.]   I. Title.
  BV265 .M67 2001
  242'.82—dc21

2001032571

01 02 03 04 05 06 07 08 09 10—10 9 8 7 6 5 4 3 2 1

MANUFACTURED IN THE UNITED STATES OF AMERICA

NGELS

His angel guards those who honor the L<small>ORD</small> and rescues them from danger.

—Psalm 34:7 TEV

O God:
   I thank you and praise you that you send your angel to guard me and take care of me. Sometimes my feet take me where I shouldn't go, and sometimes my tongue says what I shouldn't say.

   Your angel is with me all the time and keeps me safe, even though I do wrong things.

Thank you for your loving care, dear Lord. Amen.

ANGER

If you become angry, do not let your anger lead you into sin, and do not stay angry all day.
—Ephesians 4:26 TEV

Dear Lord Jesus:

You know how mad I got today when I found all my toys moved. You know how I like to keep my things all together in their own special places.

When I got angry, I just felt like kicking and yelling at everyone. I know this is not the way you want me to behave. Please forgive me for being so angry today, and help me to control my anger tomorrow.

Thank you, Jesus. Amen.

Bible

No prophecy of Scripture came about by the prophet's own interpretation. . . . but men spoke from God as they were carried along by the Holy Spirit.

—2 Peter 1:20, 21 NIV

Thank you for the Bible, God, your written Word to us.

You spoke to your people long ago, and some men wrote down what you told them. We can read those words in the Bible. Thank you that the Bible is true and that we can trust it.

Thank you for the brave people who put it in English, and those who printed it, so that we can read it for ourselves. Bless the people who put the Bible in other languages today. Amen.

Body

I urge you, brothers, in view of God's mercy, to offer your bodies as living sacrifices, holy and pleasing to God—this is your spiritual act of worship.

—Romans 12:1 NIV

Good morning, Jesus!

I'm so happy today because I can run and jump and tumble and ride my bike and sing, and do lots of things with my body.

Thank you, Jesus, that you made me so strong and healthy. Help me to look after my body, keeping it clean and eating the right foods, so that I can be the best person I can be for you. Amen.

BROTHERS

There is a friend who sticks closer than a brother.
—Proverbs 18:24 NIV

Jesus, I want to talk to you about my brother.

When he has been away for a while, I am so happy to see him home again, but then in no time we seem to start fighting with each other.

I love my brother, and I know he loves me. Please help us, Jesus, to show each other our love and to be kind and patient with each other. Amen.

CHRISTMAS

When they saw the star, they were overjoyed. On coming to the house, they saw the child with his mother Mary, and they bowed down and worshiped him.

—Matthew 2:10, 11 NIV

Dear God:

Thank you for sending your Son to our earth. When I look at the sky at night and see so many stars, I wonder how those wise men knew which one to follow. I wish I could have been there when they gave their precious gifts to the baby Jesus.

Help me to remember to be thankful for the gifts that I get this Christmas. Help me to give myself to you.

Thank you for loving me. Amen.

CHURCH

I was glad when they said to me, "Let us go to the LORD's house."

—Psalm 122:1 TEV

Dear God:

Thank you that we have a place where we go especially to worship you. Sometimes it's hard for me to sit quietly and think about you, but I do try. I love to sing the songs that make me feel happy. It is fun when people shake my hand and bless me.

When the Communion is served, I think about Jesus dying on the cross for my sins.

Thank you for my church, and for Jesus' love. Amen.

Country

Happy is the nation whose God is the Lord.
—Psalm 33:12 TEV

Thank you, God for our wonderful country, where people can be free. Thank you for the native people, who seem to know so much about the country. Forgive those who were so cruel to them.

Thank you for the brave explorers, who followed rivers and crossed mountain ranges and deserts. Thank you for the immigrants who came to this country, and worked so hard. Thank you for the people who have come from many places in the world to make their homes here.

Help us to live together happily, and to work together to make our country great. Amen.

Dad

My child, pay attention to what your father and mother tell you.

—Proverbs 1:8 TEV

Thank you, God, for my dad. He works very hard so that we can have a nice home and good food to eat.

I really like it when I'm in bed, and he comes and talks quietly with me. He helps me understand lots of things.

Please help other girls and boys who don't have good dads like mine. Help them to know you as their loving Father. Amen.

DEATH

He will wipe every tear from their eyes. There will be no more death or mourning or crying or pain.
—Revelation 21:4 NIV

Dear Lord Jesus:

Please comfort my grandma today. Grandpa has died, and we all feel very sad. We are glad that he is in heaven with you, but we will miss his happy face and all the fun things he did with us.

Thank you that your Word tells us that one day there will be no more sickness and death and tears. Please help me not to be frightened of death. Amen.

Easter

The soldiers took charge of Jesus. Carrying his own cross, he went out to the place of the Skull. . . . Here they crucified him.

—John 19:16-18 NIV

As I sat looking into the fire last night, the coals looked like a picture of your cross on the hill. It reminded me that you died on that cross to forgive my sins and make me a child of God.

Thank you for dying for me, Lord Jesus. And thank you for coming alive again, so that I can live with you forever. Amen.

Enemies

Love your enemies, do good to those who hate you.
—Luke 6:27 NIV

Dear Lord Jesus:

Today I had a really bad time at school. You know that person who is always being mean to me? Well, I got so mad that I just felt like hate was making me sick.

Your Word tells me that I should love my enemies, and pray for people who do bad things to me. It's very hard to love this person, Jesus, but when I think about it, I guess you can love her through me.

I pray that you will help me love her and make her happy. Amen.

Failure

The Lord turned and looked straight at Peter. Then Peter remembered the word the Lord had spoken to him: "Before the cock crows today, you will disown me three times." And he went outside and wept bitterly.

—Luke 22:61, 62 NIV

Dear Lord Jesus:

When Peter said that he didn't know you, you just looked at him, and he realized that he had done wrong. He was sitting quietly by the fire, just wanting to be near you, when people recognized him as your follower.

There are times when I don't do what I promise. There are times when something is just too hard for me, and I can't do it. These are times when I cry, just as Peter did.

Help me, Lord Jesus, to learn from these failures and to keep on following you. Amen.

FEAR

When I am afraid, I will trust in you.
—Psalm 56:3 NIV

Dear God:
There are so many things I'm scared about:
the big dog I have to pass each day;
the big kids who tease me and try to trip me up;
being sent to my room alone when I've been naughty;
the strange noises on a dark night;
the flash of lightning and the crash of thunder.

Help me to think of your love, dear God, when I am afraid. Be near me, I pray, because Jesus loves me. Amen.

FRIENDS

Friends always show their love. What are relatives for if not to share trouble?

—Proverbs 17:17 TEV

I thank you, Lord Jesus, for my special friends.

When I get into trouble at school, they are kind to me and make me feel better. Help me to love my friends and help them, too.

Some people are very lonely, and don't have many friends. I pray that I will remember to be kind to them and love them. Amen.

GOD

Whoever does not love does not know God, because God is love.

—1 John 4:8 NIV

Dear God:

It is very hard to know who you are or what you are like. I can't see you or hear you or touch you.

The Bible says that you are love. I know about love; that's when I feel all warm and safe and happy inside. So I can understand you and feel close to you.

Thank you for loving me so much. Amen.

GRANDPARENTS

The length of our days is seventy years—or eighty,
if we have the strength.

—Psalm 90:10 NIV

Dear God:

Thank you so much for my grandparents.

When they come to visit they always give me hugs and listen to my stories. They tell me about things they did long ago, and they teach me lots of little things from your Word.

When I stay with them, I have special things to eat and special things to do with them. Please bless my grandparents, Lord, and help me to be kind to them.

Thank you, God. Amen.

Happiness

Being cheerful keeps you healthy. It is slow death to be gloomy all the time.

—Proverbs 17:22 TEV

Happiness is being able to laugh so much that I roll around on the floor and hold my sides because it hurts so much. Happiness is being able to laugh so much that tears roll down my cheeks.

Happiness is being able to laugh so much that I gasp for air as I collapse in a heap. Happiness makes me feel so clean and strong and healthy.

Thank you, Jesus, that you can make me so warm and happy inside. Amen.

Holidays

Be at rest once more, O my soul, for the LORD has been good to you.

—Psalm 116:7 NIV

Thank you, Lord Jesus, for holidays.

It's great when we can have extra time together as a family. Dad plays games with us, and Mom reads us stories. We talk about things that are important.

When we drive along, we see the trees and mountains and beaches.

We praise you for all the great things you have made, and we thank you that we can enjoy our time together. Amen.

Honesty

They are those who, hearing the word, hold it fast in an honest and good heart, and bring forth fruit with patience.

—Luke 8:15 RSV

Dear God:

Sometimes it's hard to be honest. It's hard to admit that it's my fault when I've done something wrong. I pray that you will help me to be strong and do what is right.

I want to live an honest life, and tell the truth, even if I do get into trouble for it. Be with me and help me, I pray.

Thank you for your love. Amen.

Hospital

Blessed is he who has regard for the weak. . . . The Lord will sustain him on his sickbed and restore him from his bed of illness.

—Psalm 41:1, 3 NIV

Dear Lord:

There are so many sick people who need your loving care. Please be with the doctors and nurses as they work in our hospitals. Help them to be patient and to know what to do as they look after the sick people.

Thank you for the people who find cures for diseases. Help them in their research.

Bless the girls and boys who are in the hospital; it must get lonely for them without their families. Help them to get better soon.

Thank you for looking after me. Amen.

IMPATIENCE

The people grew impatient on the way; they spoke against God and against Moses, and said, "Why have you brought us up out of Egypt to die in the desert?

—Numbers 21:4, 5 NIV

Lord God:

How you must have been angry with your people when they grumbled and got so impatient! It's no wonder you sent snakes among them. When they finally said they were sorry and turned back to you, you helped them and saved them.

I get impatient when things don't go the way I want them to. Please forgive me when I grumble, and help me to look to you and be happy.

Thank you for sending Jesus for me. Amen.

JEALOUSY

Israel loved Joseph more than any of his other sons . . . and he made a richly ornamented robe for him. When his brothers saw that their father loved him more than any of them, they hated him. . . . His brothers were jealous of him.

—Genesis 37:3, 4, 11 NIV

Dear God:

Please forgive me when I am jealous. It is like fire burning me up, when I wish I had something someone else has. I know you are sad when I get jealous.

I know there is so much for me to be happy and thankful about. Please help me to remember all the good things you give me, and not to be jealous.

Thank you, God. Amen.

JESUS CHRIST

Jesus grew both in body and in wisdom, gaining favor with God and people.

—Luke 2:52 TEV

Dear Lord Jesus:
When you went to Jerusalem for the feast of the Passover, you must have loved talking to the teachers. You knew so much about God's Word that you surprised everyone. When your mother found you, she took you home to Nazareth, where you obeyed your parents and people loved you.

Help me to grow to know more about you. Help me to obey my parents, and to be loving like you, Lord Jesus. Amen.

KINDNESS

Be kind and compassionate to one another, forgiving each other, just as in Christ God forgave you.
—Ephesians 4:32 NIV

O God, I thank you that you are so kind and have forgiven me all the bad things I have done and thought.

I know you must be sad when you see how awful people are, and how they hurt each other. I pray that you will give me a kind heart and help me to love my family and the people I meet every day.

Make me loving like Jesus. Amen.

KNOWLEDGE

The fear of the LORD is the beginning of knowledge,
but fools despise wisdom and discipline.

—Proverbs 1:7 NIV

Dear God:

I'm not really afraid of you, because I know you love me. I want to do what pleases you.

Your Word tells me to obey my parents and to learn good things from them. Help them to trust you and learn from you, too.

Bless our family as we follow you. Thank you, Lord. Amen.

Loneliness

Turn to me, LORD, and be merciful to me, because I am lonely and weak.

—Psalm 25:16 TEV

Dear Lord Jesus:

It sometimes seems as if I am always left alone, and there is no one who will be my special friend. Everyone is busy, and they don't seem to have time for me.

When King David was lonely, he prayed to God. I ask you now to be with me and help me.

Thank you for listening to me, dear Jesus. Amen.

Love

Dear friends, let us love one another, for love comes from God.

—1 John 4:7 NIV

Dear God:

Love comes from you, so I pray that you will help me to love others. I pray that people will know you, so that they will learn to love, too. Many people in the world are sad, and many people need lots and lots of love.

Help me to love people who are not very lovable. Your love makes us happy.

Thank you, dear Lord. Amen.

Missionaries

Jesus came to them and said, " . . . Go and make disciples of all nations, baptizing them in the name of the Father and of the Son and of the Holy Spirit, and teaching them to obey everything I have commanded you."

—Matthew 28:18-20 NIV

Dear Lord Jesus:

When you were here on earth you told your disciples to go to people everywhere and tell them about you. Even though I can't go to other countries, Jesus, I do try to tell people about you here.

Bless all those people who go into the jungles and deserts, and to the mountains and cities, to tell the sad and lonely people that you love them. Please make sure the missionaries have enough food and money, and help them to be loving.

Thank you, Jesus. Amen.

MOTHER

Honor your father and your mother, so that you may live long in the land the LORD your God is giving you.

—Exodus 20:12 NIV

Please bless my mom, Lord Jesus.

She is always busy doing our washing and fixing meals and looking after the family. Help her to find time to listen to me and talk with me. Help her to find time to listen to you and talk with you, too.

I pray that you will help her to laugh more and play with us.

Bless my mom—she's special. Amen.

New year

Let us throw off everything that hinders and the sin that so easily entangles, and let us run with perseverance the race marked out for us. Let us fix our eyes on Jesus.

—Hebrews 12:1, 2 NIV

Hello, Lord. Today is the first day of the New Year. Thank you for keeping me safe and helping me last year. Sometimes I was lonely and scared, but I know you were with me.

The Bible says we are in a race, and we should look toward Jesus at the finish line. I pray you will help me keep my eyes on Jesus all through this year.

Thank you for sending Jesus. Amen.

No

Flee the evil desires of youth, and pursue righteousness, faith, love and peace, along with those who call on the Lord out of a pure heart.

—2 Timothy 2:22 NIV

Hello, Lord.

I am not allowed to say "No" very often, am I? When Paul was writing to his young friend Timothy, he told him to say "No" to things that he might have been tempted to do that were wrong.

Help me, Lord, to say "No" to doing wrong things, and help me to be a good friend to those who love and trust in you. Amen.

Obey

Children, obey your parents in everything, for this pleases the Lord.

—Colossians 3:20 NIV

Dear Lord:

Sometimes it's really hard to obey my parents and do just what they ask me to do. Help me to remember that I am pleasing you when I obey my parents.

You know that so often I just want to do what I want to do, and that it's not always best. Please forgive me and help me to obey Mom and Dad.

Thank you for helping me, Lord. Amen.

Other People

Come, let us go down and confuse their language so they will not understand each other.

—Genesis 11:7 NIV

Dear God:

When I grow up, I would like to learn to speak other languages, so that I can tell people about your love in their own language. When people look different and have different ways of dressing and eating, it is hard to understand them.

Bless the people who have come to this country so that they can be free and happy. Help me to be kind and loving to those who are different from me.

Thank you for Jesus' love. Amen.

Outdoors

How clearly the sky reveals God's glory! How plainly it shows what he has done!

—Psalm 19:1 TEV

Dear Lord Jesus:

Yesterday I went for a drive in the country with my grandma.

The mountains were gray, and there were clouds over the tops. There were rows of green grapevines on the hillside. We saw some black cattle grazing in the fields. A hawk was high up in the sky.

My grandma talked to you, Lord Jesus, as we drove along. We love being outdoors, and we love you, Lord.

Thank you for a happy day. Amen.

PETS

God made the wild animals according to their kinds, the livestock according to their kinds, and all the creatures that move along the ground according to their kinds. And God saw that it was good.

—Genesis 1:25 NIV

Dear Lord Jesus:

Did you have a dog or a cat for a pet when you were little? I can just imagine you sitting in the carpenter's shop among the wood shavings, playing with a fluffy dog. I know you would be kind to it, and make sure it had food and water every day.

Help me to care for my pet and love it. Amen.

POLITE

A gentle answer quiets anger, but a harsh one stirs it up.

—Proverbs 15:1 TEV

Dear God:

Why do I always have to be polite?

Grown-ups keep saying I should say "please," "thank-you," "sorry," "excuse me." I guess it's better to say those things than to shout and push.

Please help me to remember to say please and thank you, and be polite to people.

Thank you for loving me. Amen.

PRAYER

Don't worry about anything, but in all your prayers ask God for what you need, always asking him with a thankful heart.

—Philippians 4:6 TEV

*G*od, I am pleased that I can talk to you about everything that happens to me.

When I am worried I can pray, and you will help me. When I am happy I love to tell you the god news. I can pray when I am in church, or sitting at my desk, or anywhere and at any time.

Thank you, God, that you love to hear my prayers. Amen.

QUARRELING

Don't have anything to do with foolish and stupid arguments, because you know they produce quarrels.
—2 Timothy 2:23 NIV

Dear Lord Jesus:

Please forgive me for arguing today. I know it wasn't nice of me to answer back, and it made my mother very unhappy.

Help me to think before I speak, then remember to say good things instead of horrible things.

I pray that your Holy Spirit will help me to be nice to my friends and family. Amen.

REJOICE

Rejoice in the Lord always. I will say it again: Rejoice!

—Philippians 4:4 NIV

I feel so happy today, Lord Jesus. My mom asked me why I had such a big smile, and I said: "I'm just happy."

There are so many things that make me happy, like walking with my dad, listening to Grandma read me a story, sitting on the river bank with my grandpa trying to catch a fish, and having a hug from my mom at night, when she says "I love you."

Help me always to be cheerful, and to make other people happy too, Lord Jesus. Amen.

Rest

Come to me, all you who are weary and burdened,
and I will give you rest.

—Matthew 11:28 NIV

What a surprise it was to wake up this morning and find that I had been asleep all night!

When I went to bed I didn't feel very well, and didn't think I would sleep at all.

Thank you, Jesus, for helping me to have a good rest. I feel well and happy this morning. Amen.

RIGHTEOUSNESS

Noah was a righteous man, blameless among the people of his time, and he walked with God.

—Genesis 6:9 NIV

Dear God:

Righteousness—this is a hard word to understand. You said that Noah was a "righteous" man; he was good and did what you wanted him to do, and he trusted in you. You helped him.

Help me always to do what is right. Thank you for sending Jesus and for making me your child. Amen.

School

A man of knowledge uses words with restraint, and a man of understanding is even-tempered.
—Proverbs 17:27 NIV

Dear God:

Thank you for my school and my teachers. Sometimes I think it's a pain having to get up and go every day, but when I get there I love to play with my friends.

In class, I learn lots of things about your wonderful world. As I learn to read better, I am discovering lots of great information. One day I might be a school teacher.

Jesus was a good teacher, and the people listened to his words.

Help me, God, to listen and learn in school. Amen.

SEPARATION

The LORD is good; his love is eternal and his faith-fulness lasts forever.

—Psalm 100:5 TEV

Dear Lord God:

My best friend told me that her dad has left home, and he doesn't want to live there anymore.

She is really sad about it, and her big brother is really mad about it. Why can't people live together happily?

Please show me how I can help to cheer her up.

Thank you, God, that you don't walk out on us or change your mind about loving us. Amen.

Sickness

Is any one of you sick? He should call the elders of the church to pray over him and anoint him with oil in the name of the Lord. And the prayer offered in faith will make the sick person well; the Lord will raise him up.

—James 5:14, 15 NIV

Dear Lord Jesus:

There are a lot of girls and boys in the hospital. Please be with the doctors and nurses who look after them, and show them what to do to help the children get well again.

When people brought little children to you long ago, you put your hands on them and blessed them. Please bless all the children who are sick, and help them to get better. Amen.

TALK

Do not let any unwholesome talk come out of your mouths, but only what is helpful for building others up according to their needs, that it may benefit those who listen.

—Ephesians 4:29 NIV

Dear God:

Thank you that you have made me so that I can think and understand and talk.

Forgive me when I have said careless and hurtful things to others.

Please help me to remember to show people your love by saying good things to them, words that are kind and helpful, and that make people happy.

Thank you for your love for me. Amen.

TEASING

The tongue that brings healing is a tree of life, but a deceitful tongue crushes the spirit.
—Proverbs 15:4 NIV

Dear Lord Jesus:

Did your brothers ever tease you? Mine does! I get so mad that I hit him, then we both end up crying. I know I shouldn't hit him, but he really does annoy me.

Please help my brother not to tease and help me not to hit back.

I know that you were patient, Lord Jesus. Help me to grow more like you. Amen.

TERRIFIED

Be strong and courageous. Do not be terrified; do not be discouraged, for the LORD your God will be with you wherever you go.

—Joshua 1:9 NIV

O Lord God:

Thank you for your promise to Joshua so long ago, when you told him to be strong and brave.

There are times when I really do get terrified, and then you remind me that you are with me wherever I go. I thank you and praise you that you help me to get over these fears, and I can grow strong in your love.

Thank you for keeping me safe with Jesus. Amen.

Understanding

The LORD gives wisdom, and from his mouth come knowledge and understanding.

—Proverbs 2:6 NIV

O Lord, who can possibly know and understand everything in the whole wide world? I certainly can't.

How can I understand about being patient and loving, about schoolwork and lessons, about wars and famine and death?

You help me to know and understand things. Please make me remember, as I grow up, to listen and pray to you when I'm trying to understand. Amen.

VANITY

Anyone who listens to the word but does not do what it says is like a man who looks at his face in a mirror and, after looking at himself, goes away and immediately forgets what he looks like.

—James 1:23, 24 NIV

Dear Jesus:

Vanity is a funny, old-fashioned word. My grandma says it when I look in the mirror too much. She says that I will become vain, always thinking about how I look.

The Bible is like a mirror; it shows us what we are really like—not nearly as nice as we think we are.

Help me to look in your Word every day to see what you have done for me, and to see how I can be like you, Lord Jesus. Amen.

VEGETABLES

Better to eat vegetables with people you love than to eat the finest meat where there is hate.

—Proverbs 15:17 TEV

It was the same old story: "No ice cream until you eat your vegetables." Well, I did eat my vegetables, and I did have some ice cream.

I really am thankful that I live in a great country where I can have lovely fresh vegetables, and eat them where people love each other. It would be awful to have even the most wonderful dinners where people hate each other.

Thank you, Lord Jesus, for giving us good food each day, and for helping people to love each other. Amen.

VIOLENCE

Violent people deceive their friends and lead them to disaster.

—Proverbs 16:29 TEV

O Lord, there is so much hurt and ugliness in our world. People shoot and kill each other with guns. Others die in terrible road and air accidents. Parents abuse their kids and each other. What can we do to stop these things? What can you do, Lord?

I pray that you will help me to bring peace and happiness, rather than violence, to my home and school, and help other people to be peaceful, too.

Thank you for giving us Jesus. Amen.

Weary

Come to me, all you who are weary and burdened,
and I will give you rest.

—Matthew 11:28 NIV

Dear Lord Jesus:

Thank you for making this wonderful promise. I pray that you will help my mom tonight, because she says she is so-o-o weary, and that we children are such a burden.

Please help her to have a good night's rest, so that she will be happy tomorrow. I love my mom, and feel sad when she is so tired.

Please bless her and help her. Amen.

WILLING

God is always at work in you to make you willing and able to obey his own purpose.
—Philippians 2:13 TEV

Hello, Jesus.

Today I helped with lots of things, and didn't complain once. Wasn't that great!

I made my bed and cleaned my room. I put the plates in the cupboard. I helped keep the baby happy. I gave Mom the clothespins as she hung out the wash. I ate all my dinner, even the peas, and now I'm ready to go to bed.

Seeing that I have been so willing to help today, do you think that I could stay up just a little bit later?

Good night, Jesus. Amen.

WISDOM

How much better to get wisdom than gold, to choose understanding rather than silver!

—Proverbs 16:16 NIV

Dear God:

It is hard to know how to behave all the time.

Will you help me to understand your Word, so that I learn more about you?

Teach me to think before I speak, to put others first, and to love people who are close to me.

Thank you for being with me, Lord. Amen.

XYLOPHONE

Sing for joy to God our strength; shout aloud to the God of Jacob! Begin the music, strike the tambourine, play the melodious harp and lyre.

—Psalm 81:1, 2 NIV

Dear God:

I love to sing and dance. When I was little, my mom used to play a tape and rock me to sleep.

Now we sit on the floor and play bands. She plays the xylophone with little sticks, and I bang the toy drum. We pretend we are marching in your army.

Thank you, God, for inventing music. It makes me happy. Amen.

Yes

Do not swear by your head, for you cannot make even one hair white or black. Simply let your "Yes" be "Yes," and your "No," "No."

—Matthew 5:36, 37 NIV

Dear Lord Jesus:

When something has happened, whatever we say to try and change it, it will stay the same.

Help me to be true and honest in all I say, so that no one will doubt me. Sometimes I feel like saying something that isn't true, so that I won't get into trouble, but I know I shouldn't.

Help me, dear Lord, to say "Yes" and mean it. Amen.

YESTERDAY

Jesus Christ is the same yesterday and today and forever.

—Hebrews 13:8 NIV

Hello, Jesus.

I'm very glad that you are always the same. Yesterday wasn't so good, and today didn't get any better. I sure hope tomorrow doesn't get any worse.

Thank you that you never change, and that you always love us no matter what we are like.

Help us to love you all the time. Amen.

YOUTH

Don't let anyone look down on you because you are young, but set an example for the believers in speech, in life, in love, in faith and in purity.
—1 Timothy 4:12 NIV

Dear God:

Sometimes it's difficult being young. People pat my head or yell at me or just ignore me. Thank you that you love me and don't think I'm stupid.

Please help me to show others that I trust in you by the kind words that I say and by the way I live.

Thank you for Jesus. Amen.

ZACCHAEUS

When Jesus reached the spot, he looked up and said to him, "Zacchaeus, come down immediately. I must stay at your house today." So he came down at once and welcomed him gladly.

—Luke 19:5, 6 NIV

Dear Lord Jesus:

I wish I had been sitting in the tree with Zacchaeus when you came to Jericho. I can just imagine how excited he was when you said you were coming to his house.

You took time to visit a man who had cheated people, and straight away he was changed and became kind and generous.

Help me to listen to what you say, Lord Jesus, and always to be honest and generous. Amen.

Zoo

And God said, "Let the land produce living creatures according to their kinds: livestock, creatures that move along the ground, and wild animals, each according to its kind."

—Genesis 1:24 NIV

Dear God:

Today we visited the zoo. I love going there because we can see lots of animals and birds and butterflies. If you stand still in the Butterfly House, the butterflies will land on you. They are so silent and gentle.

How did you ever think of all the wonderful creatures you made?

I love to read books about the animals and birds you made. Perhaps I can help save some of these animals from extinction one day.

Thank you for creating these special animals, God. Amen.

God likes you to talk to him every day. Say thank you to him, and tell him what you need.